The Scientist's
Guide to Physics™

Discovering the
Speed
of
Light

CHARLES J. CAES

ROSEN
PUBLISHING®

New York

To Karen, always there!

Published in 2012 by The Rosen Publishing Group, Inc.
29 East 21st Street, New York, NY 10010

Copyright © 2012 by Charles J. Caes

First Edition

All rights reserved. No part of this book may be reproduced in any form without permission in writing from the publisher, except by a reviewer.

Library of Congress Cataloging-in-Publication Data

Caes, Charles J.
Discovering the speed of light / Charles J. Caes.—1st ed.
    p. cm.—(The scientist's guide to physics)
Includes bibliographical references and index.
ISBN 978-1-4488-4699-3 (lib. bdg.)
1. Light—Speed—Juvenile literature. 2. Light—Speed—Measurement—Juvenile literature. I. Title.
QC407.C339 2012
535—dc22

2010048426

Manufactured in the United States of America

CPSIA Compliance Information: Batch #S11YA: For further information, contact Rosen Publishing, New York, New York, at 1-800-237-9932.

3424

Contents

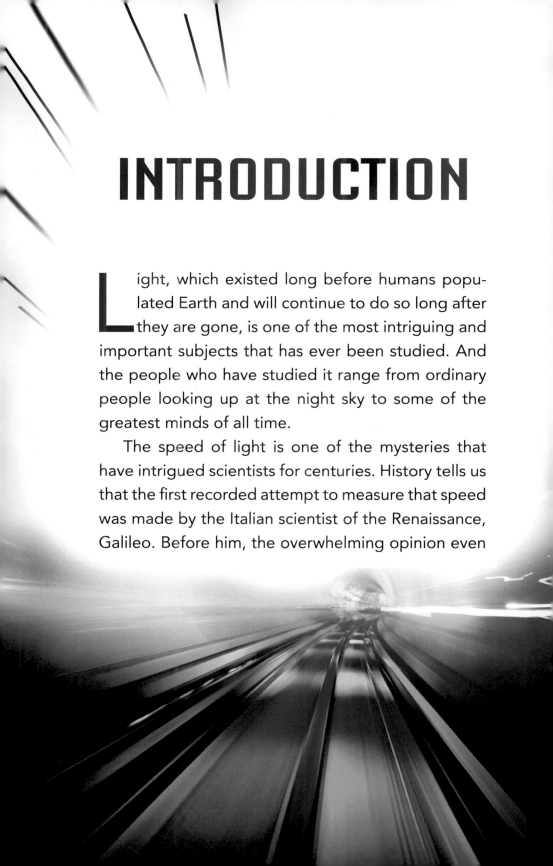

INTRODUCTION

Light, which existed long before humans populated Earth and will continue to do so long after they are gone, is one of the most intriguing and important subjects that has ever been studied. And the people who have studied it range from ordinary people looking up at the night sky to some of the greatest minds of all time.

The speed of light is one of the mysteries that have intrigued scientists for centuries. History tells us that the first recorded attempt to measure that speed was made by the Italian scientist of the Renaissance, Galileo. Before him, the overwhelming opinion even in the highest ranks of science was that it was infinite and therefore immeasurable. Chances are, however, that even in ancient times, astronomers, astrologers, and other inquiring minds driven by burning curiosity would have tried to measure it. How far away were the sun, the moon, the billions of stars? How far away were the other planets? Was it possible to measure that distance? If so, how?

Galileo was the first to try to measure the speed of light. His support of Copernicus's theory of a sun-centered solar system got him in trouble more than once with the Catholic Church.

Today, we know that light from the sun takes around eight minutes to reach Earth through the research of not just one but many inquiring minds and over a span of several hundred years. In modern times, scientists apply this discovery to new technology. Even today, researchers are continuing to explore ways to harness light and its energy.

Because the quest for the speed of light cannot be fully appreciated unless it is seen in terms of centuries of misunderstanding about light, this book begins long before the first experiment with speed took place, when men and women still believed that the eye generated light. This book will look at the people who first studied light, the first people who tried to measure it, the people who have applied the science of light to some of the great discoveries of the past, and the people who are studying light and its energy today.

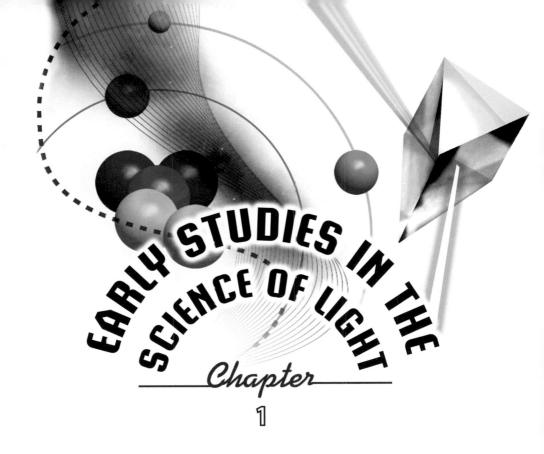

EARLY STUDIES IN THE SCIENCE OF LIGHT

Chapter 1

The speed of light was never a major question for science in ancient cultures. Almost everyone believed that the answer was obvious. Light traveled at infinite speed. How could anyone doubt that? The sun rose and its light spread immediately to all visible areas. The moonlight was there and you never saw it coming.

It wasn't so surprising a view. The speed of light isn't easily deduced from reflection or refraction, and relatively sophisticated technology is needed for its measurement.

This doesn't mean that early cultures, such as those in Egypt, the ancient Near East, and the New World, had no interest in unraveling the mysteries of

light. They did study its optical aspects. One of the earliest astronomers whose name we know was the Egyptian vizier Imhotep, who lived about 2600 BCE. Archaeologists have uncovered evidence of astronomical observatories in Mayan ruins that date to about 800 CE. And there's some evidence that sites such as Britain's Stonehenge, which dates to the first millennium BCE, may also have been used, at least in part, as an astronomical calendar.

Historians tell us the first recorded attempts to develop a science of light come from about 550 BCE, from classical Greece. The philosopher Empedocles (495–435 BCE), for instance, claimed that the eye emitted light to an object and thereby sensed it.

DEMOCRITUS

But the first to be truly analytical about the science was the philosopher-scientist Democritus. He was born in Abdera, in Thrace (in modern-day Greece), though the date of his birth may be 470 or 460 BCE,

In addition to being a doctor, high priest, scribe, pyramid architect, and advisor to King Djoser, Imhotep was also one of the earliest astronomers.

MAGI

Magi (singular: mage) also turn up, of course, as the Three Wise Men of the New Testament. The word is at the heart of our English words "magic," "mage," and "magician," and indeed many did believe that the Magi could perform powerful magic. But what the Magi of King Xerxes' court were teaching Democritus was science, not spells.

and possibly even 490 BCE. He was born into a noble, wealthy family with close ties to Greece's enemy, Xerxes, king of Persia. In fact, it was thanks to Xerxes' gratitude for his father's aid that Democritus had the chance to be taught science and philosophy by Persian Magi, or wise men.

After his father's death, Democritus became a wanderer, traveling over much of what was then the known world: Egypt, India, and the lands in between. When he returned to Abdera, he was penniless and supported himself by his wits, giving public lectures on philosophy, on the uses of various plants, and on such natural phenomena as the weather. In fact, Democritus could forecast changes in the weather so well that people began to think he could predict the future.

But Democritus didn't want to be a public figure. What he was, first and foremost, was a philosopher and a scientist whose ideas about the physical world were always based on observation and fact. He proposed that the eye consists of water and that it is able to see because it can "mirror" light traveling through the air from luminous objects. By "mirror," he meant reflect. The way he understood it, air disperses light in just the right way so that the eye can absorb it.

Democritus was a lot closer to the truth than anyone of his time could imagine. Images are formed when either generated or reflected light enters the eye. The air, however, plays no part in carrying images to the eye, nor does water. They may alter the path of light as it passes through them, causing such things as refraction or reflection, but light needs no medium for its propagation and will speed along even faster in a vacuum.

Democritus also taught that all things were made up of atoms, which he said were invisible particles consisting of the same matter but varying in size, weight, and shape. The way that they behave in relation to each other is responsible for all that we know of the world and the things that exist in it. Atomic theorist that he was, Democritus would have been pleased to

The Democritean Universe consisted of Earth and other planets in the center, surrounded by the heavens, which contain the stars, and beyond that, chaos.

learn that light is indeed caused by just such interactions as he imagined. Light is actually produced when overly energized electrons interact in their overcrowded "neighborhoods" and release their excess energy.

But Democritus much preferred a life that left him time to think. When he did attend public gatherings, he showed such sarcasm that he was nicknamed "the mocker," or "the Laughing Philosopher." Folklore surrounds his life: he was said to be eternally hunting the mythical philosopher's stone and to have blinded himself to better focus his thoughts inwardly. Neither story is true. It is true that he lived to be nearly a hundred, convinced that the secret of happiness and long life lay in possessing an even temperament.

It seems to have worked for Democritus, who died in 370 BCE.

Aristotle

The next important figure in the study of light was another philosopher and scientist, Aristotle. He was born in 384 BCE, in the seaport town of Stagirus in Thrace, the son of the court physician to King Amyntas of Macedonia. When Aristotle's father died, the boy was sent to Athens to further his education. Athens at the time was both a bustling, cosmopolitan city and the Greek center of learning. There, the young Aristotle studied with some of the great thinkers of the time, including Plato. He might have gone on to teach as Plato's successor, but Aristotle's ideas were considered too wild, and he was asked to leave. After some traveling and attempts to settle down, Aristotle returned to Macedonia under King Phillip and was made the tutor of the boy who was to become Alexander the Great.

When Alexander went off on his conquests, Aristotle was left idle. He decided to return to Athens, where he set up his own school at the Lyceum. There he taught his scientific ideas and his philosophy for thirteen years, and continued his own studies.

One of the many subjects that interested Aristotle was animal anatomy, and he wrote a treatise on the subject, *On the Parts of Animals*. In the process of writing it, Aristotle realized there was no physical evidence to support the theory Empedocles had created a hundred years before, about eyes projecting light. After all, the eyes of animals were similar to those of men, and he had never seen proof that they could project light. Besides, Aristotle wondered, if light were generated from the eye, how did one account for the fact that no one can see in the dark? Empedocles himself had to be unsure of his theory, for "he sometimes wrote that light is generated to the eye from objects outside of it." This second idea couldn't be correct, either. If light were generated by outside objects, how did it find its way to the eye?

The problem wasn't so much proving Empedocles wrong as it was discovering a believable theory to replace it. Aristotle turned to Democritus's work. He mistakenly believed that Democritus was correct in his opinion that the eye is made of water. "Facts of actual experience show this to be so," Aristotle said. "The watery nature of its parts is easily recognizable; and the substance that flows from the eyes is clearly water." But he disagreed with essential points. "Of all the elements that might bring light to the eye, it is probably water and not air as Democritus taught." And, if vision were the result of mirroring, Aristotle

wanted to know, why did not all objects capable of reflection have vision?

As he wondered about light, Aristotle also had to wonder how light came to us from the stars. In what medium did Earth, sun, and stars move? He postulated a substance he called "ether," or "aether," though there was no way to prove that it existed.

What Aristotle couldn't have known was that the idea of "ether" was to intrude on scientific thinking for over two thousand years!

Aristotle's friend and teacher, Plato, was a true Athenian: he was born in that powerful city-state in 427 BCE to wealthy parents whose families had lived in Athens for generations. But he was also a combination of aspects that may seem odd to the modern reader. Plato was a warrior who was in military service from 409 to 404 BCE, fighting in the Peloponnesian War between Athens and its rival city-state, Sparta. He was a diplomat who tried to bring Syracuse into an alliance with Athens. And he was, as we best know him, a philosopher and scholar who founded a school named after the grove of Academos in which it stood: the Academy.

The Greek philosopher Aristotle came up with the theory of ether, or "aether," a medium in which he speculated the stars, sun, and planets moved.

PLATO AND THE THEORY OF ATLANTIS

Plato was also an author who created a controversy that continues to this day: he told of an island whose inhabitants were amazingly advanced in all ways, but which sank beneath the waves. He called this island Atlantis. Was he thinking of the real island, Thera, now called Santorini? After a volcanic eruption, which occurred around 1500 BCE, the center of Thera sank and much of the rest of it was destroyed. Was Plato telling a true history of the vanished people of Thera? Or…was he just making it all up?

Among the subjects studied and discussed at the Academy were mathematics and many of the sciences. Plato, who often disapproved of Democritus's theories, had a traditional view of the sense organs in that he believed they were active rather than passive. He held on to the idea that the eye emitted light, even though he knew this didn't account for the inability to see in the dark. There might be a source of light outside the eye, Plato concluded, but he could not figure out how it might find its way to the eye—unless there were two sources of light! One must be inside the eye and the other outside, each controlled by some fundamental force in nature. Plato further stated that at night, when the outside rays were quenched by darkness, rays from the eye weren't strong enough for sight. During the day, both sources of light were able to connect, and so there was vision.

Aristotle found all the current theories lacking, though he knew that Democritus was at least right in believing the eye was a passive organ. But how did light find its way to the eye? Aristotle concluded that light neither traveled to nor from the eye but was, rather, a separate medium. In his work *Animals*, he wrote that vision "is of the nature of water and must be in order to enter the brain, which is itself a watery substance." He believed there were invisible drops of liquid in the air and these carried light to the eye. This optical relationship between the drops of water and light continued until heat or some other process caused the liquid to dissipate.

Plato died in 347 BCE, in Athens, but his Academy survived.

Then Alexander the Great died in 323 BCE. That was the end of Aristotle's days of study, since anyone connected with Macedonia was suddenly out of favor.

PLATO'S ACADEMY

Plato's Academy **not** only outlived its founder, it survived all the way to 529 CE, when the Christian emperor Justinian finally closed it down as a "pagan establishment." At nine hundred years old, the Academy holds the record of being the longest-lasting university!

Aristotle fled Athens so that, as he said, "the Athenians might not have another opportunity of sinning against philosophy as they had already done in the person of Socrates." Socrates, condemned to death for the crime of being too "dangerous" a thinker, had been forced to drink hemlock, a natural poison.

The strain of his escape may have been too much for Aristotle. Less than a year after his escape, in 322 BCE, the philosopher-scientist was dead.

Meanwhile, though, other thinkers were at work. Aristotle's theory evidently did not put the question of light to rest, for in the first century BCE, a poet and scholar by the name of Titus Lucretius (99–55) was still concerned with it. In Book IV of his *On the Nature of Things*, Lucretius showed a preference for Democritus's theory over Aristotle's, writing that "there are bodies that strike the eyes and provoke vision." Still needed was some hard evidence that could lead to a breakthrough theory.

It wasn't to appear until the ninth and tenth centuries CE, and it came from the Middle East.

MIDDLE EASTERN SCIENTISTS

Al-Kindi (813–875 CE), an astrologer as well as a philosopher, assumed that light from any source would have the same behavioral patterns as starlight. But al-Kindi, whose treatises were well known in the non-Arab world, was unlucky to have lived under the rule of Mutawakki, a caliph so suspicious of scholars, particularly philosophers, that he confiscated private libraries, including that of al-Kindi.

More fortunate was Ibn al-Haitham, also known as Alhazen. Alhazen, whose full name was Abu Ali Hasan Ibn al-Haitham, was born in Basrah in 965 CE and educated in both his home city and in the capital city of Bagdad, in what is now Iraq. He then traveled to Egypt and what would later become Spain, learning all he could about the science of physics in general and optics in particular. Much of Spain had been conquered three centuries earlier by an Islamic invasion from Morocco led by the Berber warlord

Tarik al-Ziyad—after whom Gibraltar (Tarik's Rock) is named. But by the time of Alhazen, although fighting between Moors and Christians remained, Moorish Spain had become a noted center of culture and learning.

When Alhazen reached Spain and found it so friendly to scholars and scientists, he settled there, spending much of his life researching optics and mathematics, as well as medicine and the proper development of scientific methods.

Not only was Alhazen one of the finest physicists of his era, his focus on optics and the way the eye and light work gives Alhazen the title of the father of modern optics. He was also his era's equivalent of a best-selling science writer, since his books were widely sold and, translated into Latin, became widely known all over Europe.

As a physician working in the field of optics, Alhazen was critical of any idea supposing that light originated from the eye, but he was well aware of how the eye can be affected by light. In his *The Treasury of Optics*, he explained that all objects are either capable of generating light or reflecting light. In either case, light from those objects finds its way

The Islamic scientist Alhazen, who lived from 965 to 1038 CE, focused his research on the subject of optics. He accurately described the human eye and the process of vision.

to the eye and allows the objects to be recognized. If it were the other way around, the eye would not experience pain when it stares for too great a time at some source of light. Alhazen also confirmed ideas of Lucretius and al-Kindi that light is projected in straight lines and in all directions simultaneously.

The idea of light carrying images to the eye had always been a problem. How could an image of immense size be reduced to the size of a light beam and still be perceived by the eye in real terms? If someone is looking at a 50-foot-long ship, how does the eye know the true size of the ship is 50 feet (15 meters) instead of the size of a light beam?

Alhazen explained that images did not need to be reduced. Every visible object, he stated, contained countless elements that gave off images of themselves. As these projections were constant and came from every direction, the eye perceived them at every turn. Alhazen also assumed that some observable tendencies of light, such as refraction, indicated that the speed of light is probably neither constant nor infinite.

Alhazen died in 1038 CE. While his ideas didn't have much of an immediate impact on European schools of thought—not in an age when Christians and Muslims were constantly at war—they would, over the centuries, have an extensive influence upon the field of optics. The great Italian artist and inventor Leonardo da Vinci (1452–1519), for instance, was familiar with Alhazen's *Treasury of Optics* even though it wasn't officially published in Latin until 1572.

But many scientists stubbornly clung to the old ideas. Among them was Robert Grosseteste (1170–1253), who had taught at Oxford and later founded the Oxford Franciscan School. Despite his extensive studies in light and vision and his use of mathematics and geometry in resolving issues in optics, he still argued that vision occurs because of projections from the eye.

Back to square one.

But one of Grosseteste's most famous students rejected his thesis and totally embraced that of Alhazen. This was the Franciscan friar Roger Bacon, whose knowledge of science was so far ahead of its time that many believed him to be a magician.

ROGER BACON

Roger Bacon was born in Somerset, England, in 1214, and as a youngster studied a mix of subjects, including music and astronomy. Since Paris was the center of learning in his day, he left England to attend the

University of Paris, earning a degree in 1241. But Bacon wanted to learn more. So he attended another important university, Oxford University, from 1247 to 1257. And that was when his interest in science was born.

No one is sure what prompted Bacon to leave Oxford when he did and enter the Order of Franciscan Friars. Possibly he was suffering from ill health at the time and wanted the security of a religious order. At any rate, being a friar didn't stop him from studying science, particularly optics, and getting in trouble with his fellow clerics, who didn't at all approve of his studies. In fact, Bacon spent some time in prison thanks to them, on the charge of putting "suspected novelties" into his teachings.

ROGER BACON, MAGICIAN

Several English folktales feature Roger Bacon, "magician," as their star, ranging from some that feature inventions such as talking brass heads to ones involving magical travel and detection.

This shouldn't be so surprising. It's not unusual for any scientist to be looked at as other than normal. After all, our own culture thinks of some scientists as "mad," and of "tampering with things man was not meant to know"!

That didn't stop him. Bacon remained a firm advocate for rigorous scientific experiment. In fact, he complained that one of the main causes of error was "men (who) have arisen in the universities who have created themselves masters and doctors in theology and philosophy, though they themselves have never learned anything of any account."

In other words, he was complaining about those who gained college degrees without having learned anything.

Unfortunately, although Bacon was so strong a proponent of scientific experiment, he sometimes assumed that his theories were so obviously correct they needed no experimental verification. At one time, he was reprimanded for recording experiments he never actually made!

Human nature doesn't change. The scientific method insists that an experiment must be able to be successfully duplicated if a result is to be taken as accurate. In the late twentieth century, two scientists claimed to have discovered the secret of cold fusion, the process used by the sun, but they couldn't offer convincing proof of how they'd done it.

Despite arguments with his superiors and problems with occasional vanity, Bacon was still a worthy scientist—and a quick thinker. He rapidly composed three works full of scientific ideas, including this one

APPOLONI[s] TYANEVS in Domitians Tim.

ROGER BACON an Inglishman.

for a telescope: "For we can so shape transparent bodies and arrange them in such a way...that the rays will be reflected and bent in any direction we might desire, and under any angle we wish, we may see the object near or at a distance."

Bacon went right on studying and teaching up to about a year before his death in 1294. He'd found enough coincidences between sound and light to believe that they were the same kind of phenomenon. He just wasn't sure what type of phenomenon that was.

That discovery would have to wait for later centuries.

Roger Bacon was a Franciscan friar, English philosopher, and scientist. In addition to his studies on the speed of light, he was also the first European to describe the process of making gunpowder.

EARLY LIGHT SPEED MEASUREMENT

Chapter
2

Among those influenced by Roger Bacon was an Italian physicist and astronomer who, unlike the friar, was more likely to be found in the field or laboratory than at his desk. He was Galileo Galilei, usually called simply Galileo, astronomer and physicist.

GALILEO

Galileo was born in Pisa, Italy, in 1564, the son of a noted musicologist, Vincenzo Galilei. Galileo didn't have the drive to become a musician. Instead, in 1581, he was sent to the University of Pisa as a medical student. At the university, Galileo became so fascinated with mathematics after hearing a lecture on geometry, he realized that he wasn't meant to go into medicine. He left without a degree in 1585.

The lack of a medical degree didn't stop him from studying. Galileo must have appreciated Bacon's belief that mathematics was the foundation of science and his teaching that experiment was the only absolute means of verification. But Galileo also admired the work of such scientists as Archimedes (287–212), a Greek mathematician and physicist who used experimentation and mathematics to confirm his theories, and Nicolaus Copernicus (1473–1543), a Polish astronomer who developed a heliocentric cosmology. This meant a solar system that revolved not around Earth but around the sun—a theory that challenged the Christian theology of the times.

Galileo began his long and accomplished career as a professor (possibly low paid) of mathematics at the University of Pisa, where he taught from 1589 to 1592.

During that time, Galileo developed an interest in the science of motion. He commented that "there is, in nature, perhaps nothing older than motion, concerning which the books written by philosophers

COPERNICUS'S HOBBY

Nicolaus Copernicus, who is called the founder of modern astronomy, was a cleric-scholar as well as an artist. His interest in astronomy was a private fascination, a hobby, which was why he could discover the "heretical" concept of Earth not being the center of the universe yet not get into trouble with church politics. He died without ever knowing what a controversy his findings would create.

are neither few nor small; nevertheless, I have discovered by experiment some properties of it which are worth knowing and which have not hitherto been either observed or demonstrated."

It was in Pisa that Galileo proved Aristotle wrong about the speed of falling objects. Legend has it that he did this by dropping two objects of different weights at the same time from the top of the famous Leaning Tower of Pisa, showing that the rate of falling for both was the same. In reality, the test was a little less dramatic to see but just as important: Galileo designed a device with an inclined plane down which he could roll two objects, measure their rate of descent, and time their landing. A similar experiment was carried out about four hundred years later by astronaut Dave Scott, commander of the 1971 *Apollo 15* moon landing. Scott dropped a feather and a hammer at the same time in the moon's low gravity, watched them land at the same time, and proved Galileo right once again!

In pursuing his studies and experiments with motion, Galileo laid the foundations for the science of dynamics. But he wasn't finished with scientific discoveries yet.

In 1592, Galileo was appointed to the chair of mathematics at the prestigious University of Padua, where he stayed until 1610 and continued to work on his experiments. His growing interest in optics led to an experiment to catch the speed of light. His idea was to bring an associate with a lantern to one hill and send a second associate to another about a mile away, then time the intervals between lantern signals. As the first lantern flashed, Galileo started his clock. When the second man saw the signal, he covered his lantern and the clock was turned off.

The task was doomed to failure; light traveled much too fast to be measured over such a short distance. But this did not convince Galileo that the speed of light was infinite, only that he didn't have the sufficient means to measure it.

In 1591, according to legend, Galileo set out to disprove Aristotle's theory that heavy objects fall faster than light ones by dropping two objects of different weights from the top of the Leaning Tower of Pisa.

When Galileo heard about a Dutch spectacle maker, Hans Lippershay, who designed the first telescope in 1608, he quickly went to work improving it. Before long, he had a 30-power telescope to aim at the moon, stars, and planets.

Astronomy has never been the same since. His telescopic studies defeated one superstition and false-hood after another. The moon was not a flat, polished disk but a world of mountains and valleys! The Milky Way was no longer just a great cloud of light but a celestial landscape populated with stars!

Then on January 7, 1610, Galileo discovered four moons of the planet Jupiter. He later suggested that because of their great distances and inevitable eclipses, they might serve as the basis for determining angular distances from east to west on Earth's surface. As it turned out, that suggestion would also lead to the discovery of a way to determine the speed of light, but not for another 65 years.

His fame as a scientist brought him to the attention of the Grand Duke of Tuscany, who gave him the title of mathematician to the Grand Duke. He traveled to Rome in 1611, where he became a member of the Academia dei Lincei, an important science academy. Within a year he found that the church wasn't as impressed as the Grand Duke had been.

Galileo lived in a time when religious ideas impacted the advance of science. True to the lessons of discovery, Galileo had confirmed findings by Copernicus that Earth is but a planet of the sun and not the center of the universe. Such an idea was against biblical interpretations and the theology of the times.

Denounced by the church, Galileo responded with the words of a noted ecclesiastical historian of the time, Cardinal Caesar Baronius (1538–1607), who taught that the Bible showed the way to God, not how God did things.

It was not a perspective appreciated by representatives of the church, and Galileo was soon brought to trial. The first fight between Galileo and the church went on for ten years, from 1612 to 1622, ending in him being forced to publish only with the church's permission. This wasn't acceptable to Galileo, who continued the argument until 1630, when he won permission to publish the work that finally got him into trouble for good: his *Dialogue* on the two chief world systems, which included that "heretical" theory of Earth revolving around the sun. In October 1632, Galileo was called before a church tribunal and forced to renounce his theory of Earth revolving around the sun. Folklore has it that he left the tribunal muttering defiantly, "Nevertheless, it moves!"

In 1633, Galileo was sentenced to house arrest at his home in Arcetri, near Florence, Italy. Even though blind and in rapidly declining health, he continued to pursue his interests in astronomy as best he could until his death at age 78 on January 8, 1642.

But science survived, as did scientific speculation.

Rene Descartes

The first of the "new" theories was the pressure theory of Rene Descartes. Born into a noble family in the

town of La Haye in the south of France on March 31, 1596, he was a sickly child who was forced to spend a great deal of time in bed. This, he said later, gave him plenty of time to think and started him on the path of philosophy and mathematics.

By age eighteen, Descartes was much stronger. For two years he had a wild time in Paris—making up, maybe, for all that enforced rest—but then gave that up, retreating to the suburbs where a man could think in peace. But he was still young, and not all the wildness had left him, so Descartes enlisted in the Dutch army in 1618. In 1619, on a battlefield in Germany, he had an amazing dream that gave him mathematical details. This dream led, two years later, after he had left the army to return to his Paris suburb, to the birth of analytic geometry. Up to that point, Descartes hadn't published anything, but a friend, Cardinal De Berulle, urged him to share his thoughts and findings with the world. So Descartes began to write, turning out studies of philosophy, mathematics, and science.

Rene Descartes, a great French philosopher and mathematician, is referred to by some as the father of modern philosophy. He agreed with Galileo that Earth revolved around the sun.

DESCARTES, HOLY MAN

When Descartes died, some people, confused about what he'd actually done in his life, decided that he had been a man of holy thoughts who should be beatified as a saint. As his body was being returned to France for burial, people snatched bits of it to keep as holy relics!

But Descartes couldn't avoid the troubles plaguing Galileo: he, too, believed that Earth revolved around the sun and made that part of one of his greatest works, *Le Monde* (*The World*). But Descartes also believed that the church was infallible. When the news reached him that Galileo had been forced to recant, Descartes had a genuine problem—which he solved by simply ordering that *Le Monde* not be published until after his death. But the world was already changing. *Le Monde* was published during his life, in 1637, without arguments from the church.

In 1649, young Queen Christina of Sweden ordered him to join her as her tutor in philosophy and mathematics. Descartes rushed to Sweden, only to die of lung inflammation on February 11, 1650. Some historians believe that his death was partially due to Queen Christina's request for her lessons to begin at 5 AM. Descartes normally stayed in bed until noon. The schedule might have been too taxing for his already fragile health.

Though Descartes is best remembered as a philosopher—he holds the distinction of having created one of the most often quoted statements: *Cogito ergo sum*, or, "I think, therefore I am"—he also had a keen interest in light and optics. Descartes argued that light was no more than pressure. It was transmitted by that theoretical medium first postulated by Aristotle, the ether. Descartes believed it filled all of space, could not be sensed, and did not interfere in any way with the mechanics of the world. This idea, based on that of Aristotle, struck scientists with such force that it continued to be treated with respect until the middle of the nineteenth century and was revisited on occasion as late as the mid-1950s. In fact, light waves do indeed exert pressure through their momentum, but this by no means indicates that light is a form of pressure.

Meanwhile, there were numerable successes in unraveling the mystery of refraction. The actual discovery of the law of refraction is credited to the Dutch mathematician Willebrord Snell (1580–1626), a contemporary of Galileo, although Descartes had come upon it independently and at about just the same time.

STEPHEN HAWKING

Stephen William Hawking was born in Oxford, England, on January 8, 1942, three hundred years to the day after the death of Galileo. Hawking spent thirty years as a professor of mathematics at Cambridge, retiring in 2009. His post was Lucasian Professor of Mathematics, which was held in 1669 by Isaac Newton.

Hawking has spent a lifetime researching the basic laws that govern the universe, including how Albert Einstein's

President Barack Obama presents Stephen Hawking with the Medal of Freedom in 2009. Hawking is one of the most brilliant scientific minds of the twentieth and twenty-first centuries.

theory of relativity proved, with fellow mathematical physicist Roger Penrose, that the universe began with the big bang and will eventually end in black holes. His book *A Brief History of Time*, which discusses these findings, has sold more than 10 million copies. He shared his theories on whether time travel is possible and whether alien life-forms exist in a 2010 Discovery Channel documentary series called *Into the Universe with Stephen Hawking*. He is considered one of the most, if not the most, brilliant minds of the twentieth and twenty-first centuries.

Without the work of Copernicus, Galileo, Newton, Einstein, and countless others, his research would never have been possible.

Refraction of light is the tendency of light to bend as it moves through different media. It bends because of the change of speed that occurs when it crosses the boundary of a new medium. Think about moving your arm in the air, then trying the same move in water. Feel the difference? The same thing happens on a much smaller scale to light. Every medium can cause a change in the speed of light, and this speed varies depending upon the density of the medium. In other words, the degree of refraction that takes place in clear desert air versus through glass won't be consistent.

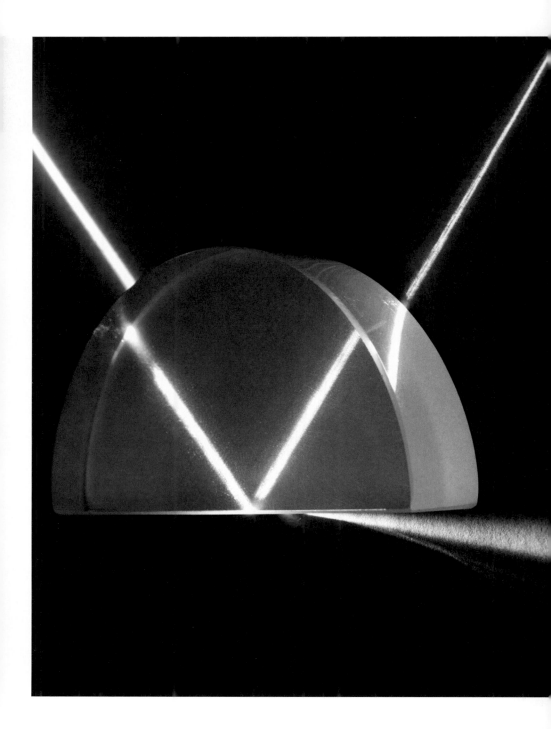

This is the refraction of light through a prism. The speed of light through the air slows as it enters the prism, changing the angle.

Optical density refers to the light-reflecting or light-transmitting qualities of the media: the fracturing of a light wave into a spectrum of color when it collides with a glass or crystal prism is an example.

But refraction of light was only part of the story. The rest would have to wait.

MORE EXPERIMENTS AND THEORIES

Chapter 3

Though astronomers and physicists were rapidly accumulating a wealth of knowledge about light and its characteristics, there was still a great deal of confusion. What was light, and how could it move with such speed?

OLE ROEMER

Olaus (or Ole) Roemer would try to answer these questions. Born on September 25, 1644, in Aarhus, Denmark, he was the son of a sea-faring merchant.

But the sea wasn't for him. Instead, the boy studied astronomy and optics in Copenhagen, where he so impressed astronomers Thomas and Erasmus Bartholin that he was assigned to edit the manuscripts of famous scientist Tycho Brahe. By 1672, he had left Denmark to became an assistant at the Royal Observatory in Paris. There, King Louis XIV appointed him to tutor the Dauphin, the royal prince, in astronomy.

In 1677, Roemer returned to Denmark to be appointed professor of astronomy and, in 1681, professor of mathematics at the University of Copenhagen. He was also astronomer royal to the Danish king. Roemer must have had an amazingly efficient and organized mind because he managed to juggle roles as teacher, master of the royal mint, harbor surveyor, and head of royal committees, and still have time for his studies in astronomy and optics.

In Roemer's time, only four of Jupiter's moons, dubbed Io, Europa, Ganymede, and Callisto after figures in Greek mythology, were known to astronomers; Galileo had discovered them in 1610. Ganymede and Callisto are larger than the planet Mercury and would ordinarily be visible to the unaided eye except for interference from light reflected from Jupiter. Io and Europa are about the size of Pluto, or one-third the size of Earth.

Ole Roemer was a Danish mathematician and astronomer. He studied the speed of light by closely monitoring the eclipses of various moons in the solar system.

Roemer attempted to verify Galileo's suggestion that the moons could be used to determine longitude. Periodically planets pass between their satellites and the sun, just as Earth does with its moon, eclipsing them. Eclipses are now predictable phenomena, but Roemer found that in the case of Jupiter's moons there was an inconsistency. Eclipses occurred a few minutes earlier than expected and at other times a few minutes later.

Roemer checked and double-checked his notes as well as the circumstances under which they were recorded, but he found nothing wrong with either. The assumptions under which he was performing his study must have been at fault then. When he checked the conditions under which each of the variances occurred, he noticed that over a period of six months, as Earth's orbit brought it closer to Jupiter, the eclipses were earlier than expected; and when Earth was more distant, they were later than anticipated. The only conclusion he could draw was that light had to be traveling at a finite speed.

It was millions of miles to Jupiter. That might be far enough to test something as fast as light. Roemer remeasured distances, orbital positions, and the intervals between eclipses, and calculated the speed of the light from the satellites to Earth to be about 191,071 miles per second (307,500 km/sec). He missed the mark but only because in his time astronomers did not know the true dimensions of Earth's orbit or have enough accurate data about Jupiter's moons.

Roemer died in Copenhagen on September 19, 1710. The scientific community wasn't ready to accept his findings. They needed further research and independent confirmation.

GIAN DOMENICO CASSINI

This would come from Jean-Dominique Cassini—or Gian Domenico Cassini, the Italian version of his name. Cassini was born in Perinald, Italy, on June 8, 1625. Although little is known about his childhood, he did study to be an astrologer. This knowledge led a rich amateur astronomer to hire Cassini to work in his observatory. There, Cassini switched his interests from astrology to astronomy, and he quickly proved himself worthy of academic honors, becoming a professor of astronomy at the University of Bologna by his early thirties. He was also working for the Bolognese government—and doing his own research at the same time. It was he who discovered four of Saturn's moons and was the first to work out accurate rotational periods of Jupiter, Mars, and Venus.

In 1693, while observing the Galilean satellites and calculating their motions, Cassini attempted to validate Roemer's experiment. Using the same method as Roemer, he measured light speed at 218,723 miles per second (352,000 km/sec), a significantly different value than Roemer's. Nonetheless, Cassini was

Gian Domenico Cassini was an Italian astronomer. He discovered four of Saturn's moons and figured out the rotational periods of Jupiter, Mars, and Venus.

Isaac Newton was the first scientist to prove that white light was actually made up of the entire spectrum of colors. He is shown here conducting the experiment using a prism.

successful in confirming Roemer's methodology. Cassini, who went on to head up the Paris Observatory and become a French citizen, died in Paris on September 14, 1715.

ISAAC NEWTON

Meanwhile, Descartes' theory of light being pressure was still popular. But it was about to face a major challenge.

Isaac Newton was born on December 25, 1642, in Woolsthorpe, a town in Lincolnshire, England, into a family of farmers. His father had died before he was born, and Newton himself was a premature, sickly baby. When he was three, his mother remarried and left her son in his grandmother's

care. That was the boy's first experience with rejection. Because he was so sickly, he couldn't play with the other children and entertained himself by making mechanical toys such as a wooden clock.

Sent to school, he was a brilliant student but, to no one's surprise, he made few friends—although as a teen, he did fall in love with the stepdaughter of the apothecary. But that was the one and only time Newton was known to fall in love at all.

When his stepfather died, Newton was taken out of school to tend the family farm. But Newton wasn't meant to be a farmer. On the advice of an uncle, he attended Trinity College at Cambridge instead, aiming for a law degree. But when he was twenty-five, a plague closed down the university, forcing Newton to study on his own. And he turned out to be what today is called a late bloomer. He suddenly discovered his passion for science and in a scant two years became a true scientist. In that brief time, he invented calculus, developed the theory of universal gravitation, and proved by experiments with prisms that white light is made up of the entire spectrum of colors. Newton couldn't accept Descartes' theory. Instead, he believed that light was made up of minute particles. It seemed, he wrote, to be a form of pressure only because it appeared to travel in straight lines and the particles traveled at high speed.

THE TRUTH ABOUT NEWTON'S APPLE

Folklore claims that Isaac Newton was sitting under an apple tree when an apple hit him on the head and gave him the idea for the theory of universal gravitation. Newton stated that no such thing had ever happened. Rather, he admitted he had, indeed, been sitting in the apple orchard when he'd seen an apple fall and gotten the idea of universal gravitation. But he firmly denied that any apple had hit him on the head!

Unfortunately, Newton still found it difficult to deal with others, particularly with fellow scientists who criticized him. The stress of trying to deal with the outside world was too much for Newton, and in 1690, he suffered a nervous breakdown from which it took almost four years to recover. When he was finally healthy again, Newton went on to government posts in London. In 1703, he became president of the Royal Society, and in 1708 he became the first English scientist to be knighted. But he never repeated the

brilliance of those two amazing years. Newton died in London, on March 31, 1727.

CHRISTIAAN HUYGENS

But just as Newton criticized Descartes' theories so, in turn, did Dutch mathematician and physicist Christiaan Huygens criticize his theories. Huygens, born the son of a diplomat on April 14, 1629, grew up in cultured surroundings, able to exercise his mind to the fullest. It wasn't a coincidence that his father was a friend of Descartes.

Huygens believed there were major flaws in the particle theory. It was obvious that light could illuminate all of space in every possible direction. Additionally, light coming from one area of a room does not interfere with light coming from another area. To Huygens, only a wave theory could explain these characteristics.

Dutch mathematician Christiaan Huygens was the first to formulate the theory that light travels in waves, similar to waves on the ocean. He is shown here with his most famous invention: the pendulum clock.

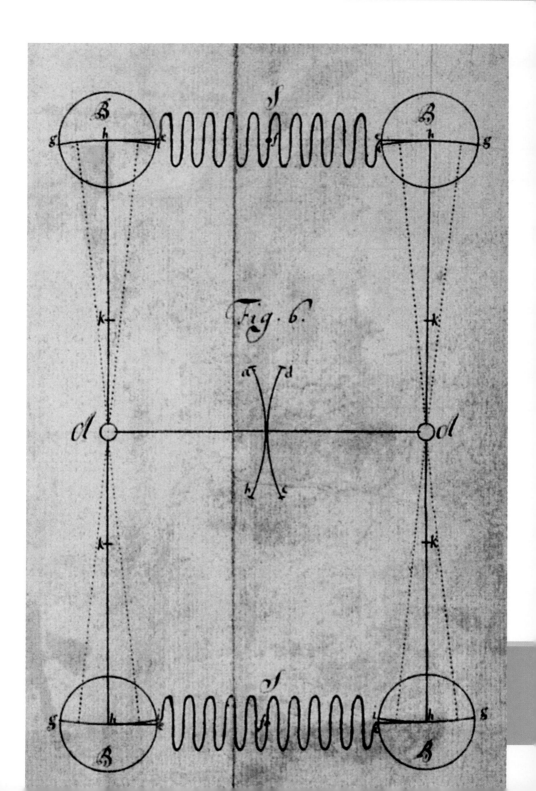

What all these intelligent men were missing, due mostly to the limits of the scientific equipment of the day, is that light waves actually do interfere with each other. In fact, when the picture on a television screen breaks up into dark and light patterns, you're quite right in calling it interference: it happens when two light waves move through the same spot at the same time.

But just what is meant by a wave? Exactly what you're probably picturing: an ocean wave. Technically, a wave is a disturbance that passes through a medium. Some waves may be higher than the others or come closer together, but they all have the same basic shape: they have their crests, the highest points, and troughs, the lowest points. Light waves—and, for that matter, sound waves—are formed in exactly the same design as ocean waves.

In addition to his study of light, Huygens patented the first pendulum clock and derived the law of centrifugal force—the force that sends objects to the outside of a spinning disk. He died on July 8, 1695.

But experiments with light, and in particular with the speed of light, continued.

This is the first model of Huygens's pendulum clock. From the time of its invention in 1656 until the 1930s, it was the most accurate way to keep time.

JAMES BRADLEY

James Bradley was born in March 1693, in Sherborne, England. Not much is recorded about his early life, though he was educated at Balliol College at Oxford, where he graduated with his M.A. in 1717, having majored in astronomy. He received further instruction in astronomy from his uncle, Reverend James Pound, who was both a clergyman and a gifted amateur astronomer. It was Pound who introduced him to Edmond Halley, after whom Halley's Comet is named, and the two became friends. Halley, in fact, recommended Bradley for the Royal Society of Astronomers in 1718. Following in his uncle's footsteps, Bradley also became a vicar in 1719 but gave that up for full-time work as a professor of astronomy at Oxford.

And it was at that post in 1724 that Bradley observed an unusual phenomenon and began a new experiment with the speed of light. He had been trying to measure the parallax of the star gamma Draconis. "Parallax" means the way a star appears to have been displaced when observed from two widely different reference points. As Earth moves along its orbit around the sun, an observed star's position changes in relation to other stars. The greatest changes are noticeable at six-month intervals because over this time span an astronomer has the advantage of being able to make observations from opposite sides of Earth's orbit, which takes twelve months (or, specifically, 365.6 days).

Bradley expected the normal slight displacement of the observed star in relation to its coordinates. But when he observed the star again six months later, gamma Draconis had apparently moved in the wrong direction! This clearly wasn't a parallax shift. What was he witnessing?

Bradley now observed a number of other stars in various parts of the sky to see if the phenomenon reoccurred or was only related to gamma Draconis. Sure enough, the phenomenon was repeated over and over again. Bradley had no choice but to conclude that the apparent displacement of Draconis could only be the result of the finite speed of light and the orbital motion of Earth.

What Bradley had observed is called the aberration of starlight (also, annual aberration); it is different from the diurnal aberration that occurs as a result of Earth rotating on its axis. The phenomenon meant that Bradley had to aim his telescope at different angles each time. The angle at which he had to reposition his telescope served as the basis for determining the speed of light, which Bradley

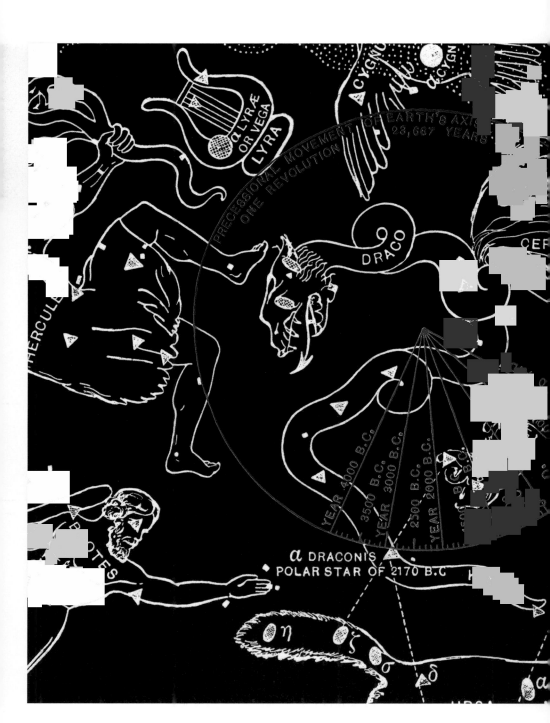

α LYRÆ OR VEGA
LYRA

α CYGNI

α CYGNI

PRECESSIONAL MOVEMENT OF EARTH'S AXIS
ONE REVOLUTION 23,687 YEARS

DRACO

CEP

HERCULES

YEAR 4000 B.C.

3500 B.C.

YEAR 3000 B.C.

2500 B.C.

YEAR 2000 B.C.

α DRACONIS
POLAR STAR OF 2170 B.C.

BOÖTES

η

ζ

δ

δ

α

James Bradley studied the orbit of Earth and how the position of the constellations seems to change because of Earth's rotation. The red circle represents the circular movement of the North Pole over thousands of years.

α URSÆ MINORII
POLARIS OR
CYNOSURA,
OF A.D.1900

calculated to be 295,000 kilometers per second (around 183,502 miles per second).

He so impressed the English astronomers by his work that Bradley was honored with the title of astronomer royal. He was only the third to hold the title; Halley had held it before him. Bradley, who married in 1744, continued his scientific studies until his death on July 13, 1762.

Meanwhile, Huygens's work received only fleeting interest during his lifetime, and his ideas took a back seat to those of Newton until the work of Thomas Young (1773–1829). Young was one of those multitalented fellows, a British physician, physicist, Egyptologist, and respected authority on the mechanics of vision and on optics. He confirmed the wave theory through detailed mathematical studies, even as the French physicist and engineer Augustin Jean Fresnel (1788–1827) was doing the same thing.

Foucault and Fizeau

The year 1819 was a good one for physicists. On September 19, 1819, Jean-Bertrand-Leon Foucault was born in Paris, France. On September 23, 1819, Armand-Hippolyte-Louis Fizeau was born in Paris, France.

Foucault, schooled at home, had a knack for mechanics, building such objects as a working steam engine when he was still a boy. He had planned to go into medicine but couldn't stand the sight of blood and switched to science instead.

Meanwhile, Fizeau's father, a professor of medi-cine in Paris, had left his son a good-sized fortune,

Armand-Hippolyte-Louis Fizeau briefly worked with Foucault to try to determine the speed of light through air and water. The two had a rocky relationship and began to work independently two years later.

leaving the young man free to study science as he wanted. He, too, had planned to study medicine, but ill health forced him to give up that idea.

In 1839, the two young scientists met, drawn together by their interest in the new science of photography and the daguerreotype. Together, they began to discuss problems in optics, heat, and light. And in 1847, they collaborated in an attempt to determine the speed of light in air and water.

But not all collaborations work out. Maybe they had too much in common, or maybe their personalities clashed. After two years of work, they quarreled one last time and went their separate ways, each continuing his own research.

As it turned out, Fizeau was the first to determine the speed of light over short distances, and he did this in the very year that he and Foucault ended their professional relationship. For his experiment, Fizeau used a mirror, a light source, and a cogged wheel. The object of his experiment was to shine light through the gaps in the teeth of the wheel and to the reflecting mirror, then reflect the beams back toward the wheel. The wheel was set so that when it was motionless, the beam went straight through a gap, struck the mirror, and was reflected back again through the same gap. By spinning the wheel at set times and speeds, Fizeau could arrange his experiment so that sometimes the reflected beam struck a cog instead of passing through a gap. The time it took the wheel to block the light with one cog, then another, was also the time it took light to make the round trip.

Fizeau calculated the speed of light to be just about 195,918 miles per second (315,300 km/sec). His measure might have been less accurate than Bradley's, but it was the first relatively successful land-based experiment.

Was Foucault jealous that his former collaborator, Fizeau, had beaten him in measuring the speed of light through air? If so, Foucault got his revenge by being the first, in 1849, to measure the speed of light through water. He used a system of mirrors inspired by an earlier experiment by Sir Charles Wheatstone (1802–1875), a French physicist well known for his work in acoustics, optics, and electricity.

Wheatstone had measured how fast an electric charge moves through a wire. He did this by using mirrors placed in such a way that he could measure the intervals between electrical sparks, which were produced by a single discharge across three spark gaps. Eventually, he was able to calculate that the charge raced through the wire at 1.3 times the speed of light, and he proposed that his experiment could also be used for determining the speed of light.

WHEATSTONE, THE INVENTOR

Sir Charles Wheatstone, who had grown up in his father's music shop, was an inventor as well as a scientist; among his creations are the concertina and early forms of the typewriter, as well as publications such as *The Harmonic Diagram*, a music theory teaching aid. He was also a professor of philosophy at King's College, London, although he made a poor lecturer due to his shyness. Because of that shyness, his fellow scientist and friend Michael Faraday usually delivered Wheatstone's scientific papers for him at the Royal Institution. Wheatstone, who never retired from his many careers, was knighted on January 30, 1868. He died of bronchitis on October 19, 1875, in the middle of a visit to demonstrate to French authorities how to improve their telegraph service.

Could it? If so, the experiment would first need improvement. As it happened, the French physicist Dominique Arago (1786–1853) had already developed the plans to do just that. Because he was less interested in determining the speed of light than he was in proving whether the waveform or particle theories were correct, he had never actually gotten around to testing his idea.

But Foucault, already impressed with Wheatstone's success and liking Arago's plan, decided to give the experiment a try. One of the results was his calculation of light speed in water. Then in 1862, Foucault used the same experiment, somewhat more refined now, to recalculate the speed of light. His system used a light source and two mirrors, one concave and stationary, and the other a flat mirror that could be spun rapidly. The equipment was set up so that when a beam of light was transmitted, it hit the rotating mirror and was reflected to the stationary mirror. The stationary mirror, in turn, would reflect the beam back along the same path to the rotating mirror. If the rotating mirror wasn't moving, it would reflect the beam back on itself.

Foucault quickly spun the flat mirror at a set speed. Because of the slightly angular rotation of the mirror, the light was reflected back to a position some distance from the starting point of the beam. Foucault measured the time it took for the light to travel from the rotating mirror to the concave mirror and back again to the rotating mirror. Then he measured the distance between the projected beam and the source position. Using a simple formula of distance and speed, he calculated the speed of light at 185,169 miles/sec (298,000 km/sec). Here was another, more efficient means for terrestrial measurement.

AU PANTHÉON
Expériences du Pendule de Foucault

Fizeau died near Paris on September 18, 1898. Foucault, worn out by a stroke that left him partially paralyzed, died in Paris on February 11, 1908.

There were still major problems regarding light to be resolved. If it did, indeed, move through some cosmic medium, what was that medium, and how could it be observed? And what, indeed, was light? That had never truly been resolved.

But new discoveries were about to be made.

James Clerk Maxwell

James Clerk Maxwell was born in Edinburgh, Scotland, on June 13, 1831, and studied there, first at the Edinburgh Academy, then at the University of Edinburgh. It was at the university that he first began studying the workings of color vision, which led in turn to an interest in color photography and light.

That he was a bit of an eccentric young man seems pretty clear: his nickname at the university was "Dafty."

Physicist Jean-Bertrand-Leon Foucault was best known for inventing the Foucault pendulum, a device that demonstrated the effect of Earth's rotation.

COLOR PHOTOGRAPHY

While James Clerk Maxwell wasn't the first to take a color photograph (that credit belongs to Sir John Herschel, who took one in 1842), he designed a three-color process for photography. But there was no way yet to use it on any wide scale. That would have to wait until 1935, when Eastman Kodak introduced its Kodachrome process, based on Maxwell's work.

Maxwell, now interested in the science of light as well, finished his formal education at Cambridge University. A year after his graduation in 1854, he published his first paper on electromagnetic theory: the theory that electric waves and magnetic waves are part of a whole, and that their oscillations (the movements of the waves) are at the heart of light.

Maxwell became a physics professor at Marischal College in Aberdeen in 1856. But when that college merged with another one, he was suddenly out of a job. In 1860, Maxwell and his wife traveled to London, where he found an appointment at King's College and settled down to work on his many interests as a

James Clerk Maxwell was a Scottish physicist, famous for his studies of light and electromagnetic waves. He also studied the composition of Saturn's rings.

physicist. In particular, he studied the composition of Saturn's rings, which he described as being composed of many solid particles—a fact that the two NASA *Voyager* spacecraft confirmed in 1980 and 1981.

Maxwell's studies led in turn to him receiving the 1857 Adams Prize for excellence, as well as to his discovery of the laws governing the movement of gases.

Maxwell continued to work on his theories of electromagnetism. In 1864, he delivered another paper to the Royal Society of London. In *A Dynamic Theory of the Electro-Magnetic Field*, he said, "We have strong reason to conclude that light itself—including radiant heat and other radiation, if any—is an electro-magnetic disturbance in the form of waves propagated through the electro-magnetic field according to electro-magnetic laws."

MAXWELL'S THEORY CHANGES THE WORLD

Maxwell's electromagnetic theory continued impressing scientists into the twentieth century. Albert Einstein stated, "This change in the conception of reality is the most profound and the most fruitful that physics has experienced since the time of Newton." Physicist Richard Feynman added, "There can be little doubt that the most significant event of the 19th century will be judged as Maxwell's discovery of the laws of electrodynamics."

This may not sound impressive at first reading, but it was a startling breakthrough about the true nature of light—and of the composition of reality. No one till then had ever realized that such fields as electricity and magnetism might be parts of a whole, and that physical reality might actually be defined.

In 1871, Maxwell became the first professor of experimental physics at Cambridge University and directed the university's Cavendish Laboratory. But his most important discovery was surely when he realized that electric and magnetic fields could be proven to be parts of a whole through only a few relatively simple equations.

However, Maxwell, trying to discover further natural laws, remembered Aristotle's and Descartes' idea of a mysterious substance called "ether" and proposed that ether was the answer for which he was looking. Surely if ether existed throughout space, it would transmit electromagnetic vibrations. Maxwell lived until 1879 without finding any clue about the existence of ether.

This triggered a series of experiments by physicists trying to measure Earth's motion through the ether, but they never could confirm its existence, either. Scientists can be as in love with their own ideas as anyone else. So sure were they that the ether existed that they thought the failures were caused not by a

Albert Michelson was awarded the Nobel Prize in Physics in 1907, the first time it would be awarded to an American. He is shown here in his lab in 1930.

lack of ether but by inherent problems with the experiments.

Then along came Albert Michelson.

ALBERT MICHELSON

Albert Michelson was born on December 19, 1852, in what is now Poland, but when he was two years old, he immigrated with his parents to the United States, settling in San Francisco, California. There, Michelson's father became a successful sea merchant.

When he was seventeen years old, Michelson, planning to be a sailor, entered the U.S. Naval Academy in Maryland. He soon found out that he was a far better scientist than he was a sailor and switched his field of study to physics. Graduating in 1873, Michelson served as the academy's science instructor from 1875 to 1879.

But he wasn't neglecting his research. In 1878, Michelson focused on what was to become his passion: the accurate measurement of the speed of light. By the 1880s, he had become determined to learn once and for all whether or not the ether existed. He would do this by comparing the velocity of light waves traveling in different directions. Since there had never yet been proof of the ether, one could assume that Earth moved through this strange medium without disturbing it. Therefore, light must be moving with greater speed with the ether than against it, or there would have been some measurable disruption.

For this measurement, Michelson designed and developed a highly sensitive interferometer, an instrument intended to split a light beam into two parts, send the parts down perpendicular paths, then reunite them. If the two light waves no longer quite matched up, patterns of dark and light stripes of interference would show up. The number of those stripes and their width would allow the most precise measurements ever made of the comparative speed of two beams of light.

What Michelson was trying to do with this experiment was measure the speed of Earth through the ether. In 1887, with his colleague, Edward Williams Morley, he set out to detect the ether once and for all.

Instead, to his dismay, Michelson proved once and for all that there wasn't any ether.

The results of his experiment sent the world of physics reeling. It was as though Michelson had just proved there was no such thing as the sun! A great deal of effort went into the attempts to disprove Michelson and Morley—but these attempts only backed up their findings.

There was no ether.

THEORIES OF THE 19TH, 20TH, AND 21ST CENTURIES

Chapter 4

One of the first scientists to challenge the old ways of thinking was the brilliant physicist Max Planck.

MAX PLANCK

Born Max Karl Ernst Ludwig Planck on April 23, 1858, in Kiel, Germany, Planck came from a family of academics, with three generations of professors on his father's side. His own interest in physics

German physicist Max Planck has been called the father of modern physics. He received the Nobel Prize in Physics in 1918 for his study of black body radiation.

and mathematics blossomed when he entered the Maximillian Gymnasium—a famous Munich educational institute—although the boy also loved music and became quite a talented pianist. But Planck chose physics as his career, since he was sure that that was where the greatest originality was yet to come.

Entering the University of Munich in 1874, the young man refused to let his professors discourage him from studying physics by their arguments that surely all the great discoveries in physics had already been made.

Planck eventually proved those narrow-sighted professors wrong. He became the first of what are now known as theoretical physicists, those who deal with the theories rather than the "nuts and bolts" of reality, and tackled a problem that had perplexed physicists in the late nineteenth century. It had to do with "black body radiation," which is just another term for thermal (heat) radiation. There isn't any physical thing as a black body. It's a theoretical "object" that is a perfect absorber of all radiation that comes to it and a perfect re-emitter of that radiation. Physicists knew that the concept of the black body should make sense, but they couldn't explain it in terms of the classical physics of the time, which depended upon a wave theory of light; the black body theory just didn't work with the longer light waves.

When Planck began studying the problem, he discovered that he couldn't create a working mathematical model unless he rethought the natures of light and energy. What if they weren't made up of continuous streams of waves after all? Planck set to work designing his mathematical models and determined in 1900 that energy was transmitted not in continuous streams of data according to the theories of current physics, but in tiny bundles, units that he named quanta. Each unit alone was a quantum—and this gave Planck's theory a name: the quantum theory.

Planck's findings at first appeared to be a contradiction. If light was still to be accepted as being a waveform, as it almost universally was by scientists, how could Planck believe that light would be emitted as quanta?

Actually, Planck was just as surprised as everybody else by his results. But no matter how often he went over them, there could be no doubt: his mathematics had been perfect. Planck pointed out to the other scientists that what he had given was a theoretical proof of how quantum theory could explain black body radiation. Whether or not quanta actually existed was another matter.

Then along came another scientist, possibly one of the greatest thinkers of the twentieth century. His name was Albert Einstein.

Albert Einstein

Born in Germany on March 14, 1879, Einstein came from an ordinary middle-class family. His father was

Albert Einstein, most famous for his formulation of the theory of relativity, is seen here in 1930. He received the Nobel Prize in Physics in 1921.

a manufacturer of electrical equipment, and a business failure forced the family to move to Munich, then to Milan. All the while the family was moving, the young Einstein showed so little intellectual ability that his parents were beginning to wonder if their son was a bit backward. He was also disruptive in class. It was only later that the truth came out. The boy had hated the rigid style of teaching that was then the norm in Germany. When left alone, he studied science and mathematics eagerly.

When his family moved to Milan, Einstein dropped out of school to join them. This lead to his German citizenship being revoked in 1896. That didn't seem to bother Einstein at all; instead of arguing, he enrolled in the Swiss Federal Institute of

Technology in Zurich. He didn't find this academic world to his liking, either, but Einstein did manage to stay with it long enough to earn his degree in 1900. He became a Swiss citizen in 1901.

In 1902, Einstein found a job in the Zurich patent office, where he remained for seven years. Maybe it wasn't an intellectual job, but it had the advantage of allowing Einstein the time he craved to study, think, and work on several important theories.

One subject that Einstein found intriguing was the work Planck was doing. But Einstein wasn't ready to reject the wave theory altogether. After all, it had offered science a means of understanding a great many peculiarities about light and energy. Still, there was no denying that some experimental results simply could not be predicted by wave theory. Alternative theories did have to be considered.

Einstein began to formulate his own. In 1905, he wrote what many people think is his greatest work: four papers, each containing vitally important theories—and altering the course of physics.

Paper number one dealt with the random movement of molecules in a solution, known as the Brownian movement after botanist Robert Brown, who had first discovered it in 1827.

Paper number two dealt with light and reinforced Planck's quantum theory. In this paper, Einstein proved the nature of light as a series of photons, Planck's quanta, and earned himself the Nobel Prize in Physics for it in 1921.

Paper number three is the most famous of the four. Taking as a given that the laws of physics hold constant in any frame of reference, Einstein proposed his special theory of relativity. In it, he explained that time and space can only be experienced in ways that are relative to each person.

What does that mean? Imagine, for instance, standing still as a train goes by and seeing a passenger in the train seem to blur with speed. Now imagine being that passenger and seeing someone who is actually standing still but seems to be rushing backward. It gets weirder. Imagine that both the person on the ground and the passenger in the train are wearing watches. Because the passenger speeding along in the train is going faster than the person on the ground, the passenger's watch is also in a slightly faster frame of existence. If the train could somehow fly at half the speed of light, we could measure a genuine difference between the time frames of the two watches.

Paper number four contains Einstein's most famous equation, $E = mc^2$ (energy is equal to mass multiplied by the speed of light squared). The paper not only makes use of this proposal, it also theorizes that nothing can travel faster than the speed of light.

Such travel, at least using the physics equations available to us now, would be impossible because the faster an object travels, the more mass it acquires, and the more energy it needs to overcome that added weight. Eventually, it would use up all the energy in the universe!

All this while, Albert Michelson was continuing his studies of light, as well as working to improve upon astronomer Simon Newcomb's studies. By 1926, at age seventy-four, he was ready to experiment. Using a 22-mile (35 km) path between Mount Wilson and Mount San Antonio in California, he came in with an average measure for the speed of light of 186,285 miles/sec (299,797 km/sec).

Michelson continued to dominate the mechanical device scene until his death in 1931. While the advance of new technology and a greater understanding of the physics of light would overshadow his methods and results, his contributions were important to the rapid advance of optical measurement.

Meanwhile, Einstein's four papers issued in 1905, when he was only twenty-six, earned him his first teaching post, a professorship at the University of Bern, Switzerland, in 1908. Einstein might have stayed in Europe, especially after winning the Nobel Prize in Physics. But by the early 1930s, the Nazi Party was rising to power.

THE THEORY OF WARP SPEED

Entering into the realm of science fiction, writers have been casually using terms like "FTL (faster than light) drives" to get their characters zipping about the universe, while *Star Trek* has invented ships that travel at "warp speed" to avoid the problem of the limitations of the speed of light.

But truth may turn out to be stranger than fiction after all. Several scientists are working on theories not to go faster than light, but to avoid it altogether. In 1994, Miguel Alcubierre, a mathematician from Mexico, published a paper theorizing how a genuine warp drive might work by distorting the fabric of space, keeping a starship out of the direct flow of time. His theory still required too much energy. But in 1999, professor Chris Van Den Broeck in Leuven, Belgium, published a paper revising the theory so that it, while still impossible to use with our current technology, required far less energy.

The word "theory" must be stressed here. However, NASA does have a department labeled "Breakthrough Propulsion Physics." There may yet be some way around the barrier presented by Einstein's theories. According to Baylor physicist Gerald Cleaver in a 2008 *Discovery News* article, if warp drive is possible, it probably will not be available for several millennia.

Einstein was Jewish. He and his family left Europe and settled in the United States. Becoming a citizen, Einstein found a home at the Institute for Advanced Study in Princeton, New Jersey, in 1933. There he stayed and worked, trying to devise a unified field theory, a theory, that is, that would prove a link between gravitation and subatomic and electromagnetic fields. To date, no one has achieved this.

Meanwhile, Max Planck wasn't as fortunate as Einstein. Planck, who loved his native Germany, never left. He had already tragically lost his wife of twenty-two years, as well as three of his four children by her. Now, he spoke out against Hitler and the Nazis but made no progress. His house was destroyed during World War II, and his last remaining son, Erwin, was implicated in the attempt to assassinate Hitler on July 20, 1944, and died a terrible death.

Planck survived the war but had lost all will to live. He died at the age of eighty-nine on October 4, 1947.

Meanwhile, in the United States, Einstein was never completely satisfied with the quantum theory. He believed it to be an "incomplete description of the individual system." But being a practical man, he also believed that scientists didn't need to worry about solving all the mysteries because laws can be "formulated within the framework of our incomplete system."

THE WIT OF EINSTEIN

Einstein, who spoke English fluently, though with a heavy German accent, proved himself both witty and very quotable.

On his theory of relativity: "Put your hand on a hot stove for a minute, and it seems like an hour. Sit with a pretty girl for an hour, and it seems like a minute. THAT'S relativity."

On knowledge and imagination: "Imagination is more important than knowledge. Knowledge is limited. Imagination encircles the world."

On himself: "I have no particular talent. I am merely inquisitive."

Einstein became a celebrity in the United States, since he perfectly fit everyone's stereotype of the scientist and had a good sense of humor about it. He died in Princeton on April 18, 1955, but even today, his image still appears on T-shirts and posters, cartoons, and commercials.

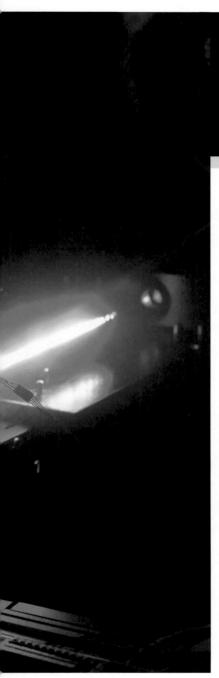

The study of light over the last several centuries has allowed humans to harness the power of light for lasers. This laser is used by manufacturers to drill, weld, and cut metal pieces.

THE SPEED OF LIGHT TODAY

Meanwhile, while Einstein had been trying to discover a unified field theory, other scientists were trying their own experiments. One type involved Kerr cells, which, upon receiving an electric charge, become high-speed shutters for light beams. The results from these experiments, however, were too inconsistent to allow for any confirmations.

Then came the laser, which itself is basically a tightly focused beam of light; the name is an acronym for "light amplification by stimulated emission of

LIGHT-YEARS

The time it takes light to travel in one year is often used as a means of measure in astronomy. For instance, at 182,282 miles/sec, light will cover just about 5.9 trillion miles (9.5 trillion kilometers) in one year. This is called a light-year. It is much easier to express these great distances in light time. For instance, the star Draconis is said to be 108 light-years away; that's the distance light would travel in 108 years—6.37526843×1014 miles (1.026 quadrillion kilometers). Often, however, for distances well beyond our solar system, the parsec is sometimes used. The parsec is equivalent to 3.2616 light-years. The distance to Draconis, then, can also be indicated as 33.11 parsecs.

Smaller units are sometimes used for distances within the solar system, such as light-second, light-week, light-day, or light-month. Astronomers occasionally use the term "astronomical unit" to give the distance to a planet. An astronomical unit is the equivalent of 499.005 light seconds.

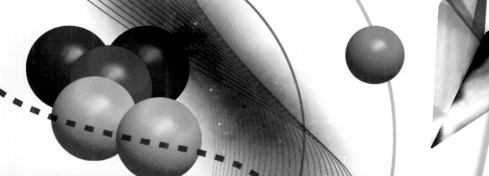

radiation." Invented in 1958, by Arthur L. Schawlow and Charles H. Townes, the laser is useful in many sciences (as well as in the modern supermarket cash register) because the light particles don't scatter. This property also makes the laser an ideal tool for precise measurements. In 1972, the National Bureau of Standards, now the National Institute of Standards and Technology, assigned a team to use lasers to determine the speed of light. The team arrived at a value of 299,792,456.2 +/- 1.1 km/s.

Subsequent experiments by other research teams confirmed the results. For the first time since Roemer measured the speed of light using the Galilean moons, values arrived at independently were in agreement. Thus, the speed of light officially became 299,272,458 km/sec, or about 182,282 statute miles per second.

How fast is that? It takes a beam of light only eight minutes to travel the 93 million miles (150 million km) from the sun to Earth. And it would take a beam of light only one second to circle Earth seven times.

But is the speed of light really constant? Can nothing really travel faster than that speed? Physicists have begun speculating that the speed of light might have been faster shortly after the birth of the universe, or that there may be two or even more versions of the speed of light, depending on which calculations of the universe are used.

In the summer of 2000, teams at the NEC Research Institute in Princeton, New Jersey, succeeded in driving a pulse of light far beyond the current expected value for the speed of light. How could this be possible?

The answer is that while Einstein's theory states nothing with mass (that is, nothing solid) can move faster than the speed of light, a light pulse has no mass and isn't bound by the same law.

But what about changing the speed of light? Is that possible?

Up to the last ten years of the twentieth century, the answer would have been no. Einstein had speculated that light might be slowed, but no one had ever been able to perform a successful experiment—until Lene Hau, a Harvard University physicist, and a team of scientists under her did exactly that in 1998. Working with a new state of matter, made up of atoms packed together tightly in very low temperatures and high vacuum, Hau and her team slowed light down to an amazing 38 miles per hour (61 km per hour). Then, in 2000, she succeeded in completely stopping a beam of light. By 2007, she was able to stop a pulse of light

Danish physicist Lene Hau, a Harvard professor, was the first person to find a way to slow down, and stop, the movement of light.

LENE HAU

Lene Vestergaard Hau was born in Vejle, Denmark, on November 13, 1959. Neither of her parents had a background in science or mathematics, but they believed in giving their daughter a good education. At first, when she began college at Arhus University, Hau was bored by physics. But she loved mathematics. When she discovered quantum mechanics, Hau became hooked on physics again through her love of math.

She earned her Ph.D. in quantum theory in 1984, and in 1988, she traveled to the United States and began her research into cooling atoms and slowing down the speed of light. She successfully stopped the speed of light in 2000. When Bertel Haarder, the Danish minister for the interior and health, visited the Hau Laboratory in 2010, he stopped a light pulse using Hau's apparatus. That year, Lene Hau was named "World Dane 2010" by global network Danes Worldwide.

and make it start again at .13 miles per hour (.2 km per hour). Her secret was a lump of atoms (called a Bose-Einstein condensate) cooled to nearly absolute zero (-459.67 degrees Fahrenheit/-273.15 degrees

Celsius). Enclosed in a steel container, this created a special type of vacuum that made slowing and stopping light possible.

The speed of light wasn't constant after all.

What does this mean for the future? It seems likely that we'll be seeing new inventions in data transfer, computers, and picture storage at the least. Beyond that, no one knows—yet.

One thing is certain: we haven't broken the laws of physics. We simply don't completely understand them!

2600 BCE The Egyptian vizier Imhotep begins his astronomy research.

813 BCE Al-Kindi is born.

384 BCE Aristotle is born.

1247 Roger Bacon enters Oxford University.

1596 Rene Descartes is born.

1638 Through Rene Descartes' research, he introduces the "modern" notion of the ether; Galileo attempts to measure the speed of light by a lantern relay between distant hilltops.

1665–1666 Plague closes Cambridge, resulting in two great years of discovery for Isaac Newton.

1675 Isaac Newton delivers his theory of light.

1676 Ole Roemer measures the speed of light by observing Jupiter's moons.

1839 Foucault and Fizeau meet.

1916 Albert Einstein publishes his paper on the theory of relativity.

1921 Einstein receives the Nobel Prize in Physics.

1988 Stephen Hawking publishes *A Brief History of Time.*

2000 Lene Hau succeeds in stopping light.

2010 *Into the Universe with Stephen Hawking* premieres on the Discovery Channel.

corpuscle A minute particle.

electromagnetic The physical quality of having both electric and magnetic properties.

energy The capacity to perform work either by motion or relative position.

ether Theoretical undetectable medium in all of space; also known as aether.

frequency The number of times a phenomenon occurs over a given period of time.

interference Patterns of high and low intensity caused by waves interacting with each other.

laser A device used to create and amplify a beam of light. The name is an acronym for "light amplification by stimulated emission of radiation."

medium Any intervening substance, such as air, water, or crystal.

meter The unit of measure equivalent to 1/299,792,458 of the distance light travels in one second.

orbit A circular or elliptical gravitational path followed by an object as it moves about another object, as in the case of Earth moving about the sun.

photon A quantum of electromagnetic radiation.

pulse An abrupt change in electrical pressure, which conveys information.

quantum An independent form of energy.

rectilinear Forming a straight line.

reflection A phenomenon that results in part of a wave having its direction changed before entering a medium.

refraction A phenomenon that results in part of a wave having its direction changed while entering a medium.

scattering The random deflection of waves as they pass through an irregular medium.

solar Relating to the sun.

stellar Relating to a star or stars.

velocity The magnitude and direction of an object.

wave A physical activity that rises or falls or moves forward or backward with periodic motion through a medium.

Canadian Association of Physicists

Suite 112, MacDonald Building
University of Ottawa
150 Louis Pasteur Priv.
Ottawa, ON K1N 6N5
Canada
(613) 562-5614
Web site: http://www.cap.ca

This association helps keep Canadian physicists informed of the latest developments.

Canadian Space Society

65 Carl Hall Road
Toronto, ON M3K 2E1
Canada
Web site: http://www.css.ca

This national nonprofit organization is made up of professionals and enthusiasts pursuing the human exploration and development of the solar system and beyond.

Center for the History of Physics

American Institute of Physics
One Physics Ellipse
College Park, MD 20740-3845
(301) 209-3100
Web site: http://www.aip.org

This nonprofit organization promotes the advancement and study of physics and its application to human welfare.

Historical Society of Princeton

Bainbridge House

158 Nassau Street

Princeton, NJ 08542

(609) 921-6748

Web site: http://www.princetonhistory.org

The museum and library are dedicated to the preservation of the history of Princeton, including a large quantity of Albert Einstein's scientific artifacts.

Museo Galileo

Institute and Museum of the History of Science

Piazza dei Giudici 1

50122 Florence, Italy

Web site: http://www.museogalileo.it

The Museo Galileo is one of the foremost international institutes on the history of science.

National Air and Space Museum

7th and Independence Avenue

Washington, DC 20580

(202) 357-2700

Web site: http://www.nasm.si.edu

The museum contains the largest collection of historic air and spacecraft in the world and is a vital center for research into the history of science and technology.

The Optical Society

2010 Massachusetts Avenue NW

Washington, DC 20036
(202) 223-8130
Web site: http://www.osa.org
Society of optics and photonics scientists, engineers, educators, and business leaders that gives them a place to share their discoveries and work together to create new innovations for the common good.

WEB SITES

Due to the changing nature of Internet links, Rosen Publishing has developed an online list of Web sites related to the subject of this book. This site is updated regularly. Please use this link to access the list:

http://www.rosenlinks.com/phys/light

Abboud, Tony. *Al Kindi: The Father of Arab Philosophy*. New York, NY: Rosen Publishing, 2006.

Adamson, Peter. *Al-Kindi*. New York, NY: Oxford University Press, 2006.

Anderson, Margaret. *Isaac Newton: The Greatest Scientist of All Time*. Berkeley Heights, NJ: Enslow Publishers, 2008.

Aristotle. *The Athenian Constitution*. New York, NY: Merchant, 2009.

Brown, Alison. *The Return of Lucretius to Renaissance Florence*. Cambridge, MA: Harvard University Press, 2010.

Clark, Ronald W. *Einstein: The Life and Times*. New York, NY: HarperCollins, 2007.

Drake, Stillman. *Galileo*. New York, NY: Sterling, 2010.

Hawking, Stephen. *A Brief History of Time: From the Big Bang to Black Holes*. New York, NY: Random House, 1998.

Heilbron, John. *Galileo*. New York, NY: Oxford University Press, 2010.

Isaacson, Walter. *Einstein: His Life and Universe*. New York, NY: Simon & Schuster, 2008.

Krull, Kathleen. *Isaac Newton*. New York, NY: Penguin, 2008.

Macfarlane, Katherine. *The Father of the Atom: Democritus and the Nature of Matter*. Berkeley Heights, NJ: Enslow Publishers, 2009.

Nardo, Don, Martin Gaskell, and Rosemary Palmer. *Tycho Brahe: Pioneer of Astronomy*. Mankato, MN: Capstone, 2007.

Robinson, Andrew. *Einstein: A Hundred Years of Relativity*. New York, NY: Sterling, 2010.

Sandys, John Edwin. *Roger Bacon*. Whitefish, MT: Kessinger, 2010.

Steele, Philip. *Isaac Newton: The Scientist Who Changed Everything*. New York, NY: National Geographic, 2007.

Index

A

B

C

D

E

F

G

H

About the Author

Charles J. Caes is the author of several books for teens on science and other subjects. He lives in Virginia.

Photo Credits

Cover, p. 4 © www.istockphoto.com/Nikada; p. 5 Stock Montage/Archive Photos/Getty Images; p. 8 Dorling Kindersley/Getty Images; pp. 12–13 Cordelia Molloy/Photo Researchers; p. 16 Vanni/Art Resource, N.Y.; pp. 23, 62–63 Sheila Terry/Photo Researchers; p. 28 © Charles Walker/Topfoto/The Image Works; pp. 34–35 *Galileo* by James Edwin McConnell/Look and Learn/The Bridgeman Art Library; p. 38 DEA/G. Dagli Orti/De Agostini Picture Library/Getty Images; p. 42 Chip Somodeville/Getty Images News/Getty Images; pp. 44–45 GIPhotoStock/Photo Researchers; p. 48 Science Source/Photo Researchers; p. 50 © Image Asset Management Ltd./SuperStock; pp. 52–53 Apic/Hulton Archive/Getty Images; p. 56 Three Lions/Hulton Archive/Getty Images; pp. 58, 73 New York Public Library/Photo Researchers; p. 65 SSPL via Getty Images; p. 70 Roger Viollet Collection/Getty Images; p. 76–77, 84–85 Keystone-France/Gamma-Keystone via Getty Images; p. 81 Michael Gottschalk/DDP/Getty Images; pp. 92–93 Mary Knox Merrill/The Christian Science Monitor/Getty Images; p. 96 Justin Ide, Harvard News Office.

Editor: Bethany Bryan; Photo Researcher: Marty Levick